JUNIOR
BIOGRAPHIES

Rita Santos

ALICIA KEYS

SINGER-SONGWRITER

Words to Know

activist A person who believes strongly in a cause and works for change.

ambassador A person who represents a group.

diverse Having many different kinds of people.

documentary A film about true events or facts.

entrepreneur A person who starts a business.

human rights The basic rights that belong to every person.

mature To grow and develop.

multiracial Having a family that is made up of people of different races.

ostracize To not include someone.

paralegal A person who works at a law office helping lawyers.

scholarship A money award that helps a student pay for school.

valedictorian The student who gives a speech at graduation and usually has the highest overall grades in the class.

CONTENTS

Alicia Keys

CHAPTER 1

THE BEAT OF THE STREET

Alicia Augello Cook performed for the very first time at the age of four. She played the role of Dorothy in her kindergarten class play of *The Wizard of Oz*. Alicia loved being onstage. That same year, she got her first television role in an episode of *The Cosby Show*. She was on her way.

NEW YORK NATIVE

Alicia was born on January 25, 1981, in New York City. She lived in a neighborhood called Hell's Kitchen. Alicia and her mother, Teresa, shared a small apartment. It had only one bedroom. Alicia had to sleep on the couch.

Alicia's father, Craig Cook, was a flight attendant. He and Teresa separated when Alicia was just two years old. For a long time, Alicia was angry at her father for leaving. The two did not really speak to each other until Alicia was an adult.

Alicia Says:
"In New York, anything goes."

Alicia's mother, Teresa, encouraged her daughter's love of music and theater.

Alicia's mother is Italian American. Her father is African American. New York City is very **diverse**. Alicia grew up around many other **multiracial** children.

A MUSICAL BEGINNING

Alicia loved the sounds of her neighborhood. It was close to Broadway. Her mother was a **paralegal**. She was also an actress. She loved taking her daughter to theater and musical shows. The family enjoyed the many different cultures of their city.

Alicia loved her neighborhood. But Hell's Kitchen could be a dangerous place. Alicia's mom wanted to keep her out of trouble. She signed Alicia up for lessons in piano, singing, and dancing. The lessons kept Alicia busy. But she still found time to hang out with her friends from Manhattan's Professional Performance Arts School. She and her friends even started an all-girl group. The group did not last long.

RECORDING ARTIST

People noticed Alicia's talent. When she was only fifteen, she got her first record deal. But the record company wanted her to change her style. They wanted her to sing more and play piano less. She liked to mix her classical

Young Alicia loved spending time on Broadway when she was growing up.

Other famous performers, like Sarah Hyland of *Modern Family*, also graduated from Alicia's high school.

piano training with the hip-hop she heard growing up. The record label didn't like the new sound she was creating. Alicia had to be true to herself. She walked away from her record deal. Alicia knew someone would like her sound.

CHAPTER 2
CREATING HER OWN SOUND

Alicia had always been a strong student. She graduated high school two years early. She was **valedictorian** of her class. In 1998 she received a **scholarship** to attend Columbia University. But Alicia wanted to focus on her music career. She did not want to go to school anymore. She left Columbia after only four weeks. She changed her last name from Cook to Keys. As a piano player, she felt the name had special meaning.

THE RIGHT DEAL

Clive Davis is a very famous record producer. When he heard Alicia perform, he knew she was special. He had been the president of Arista Records and had recently started J Records. Davis liked Alicia's sound. He signed her to a record deal. Her first album, *Songs in A Minor,* was set to be released in June 2001.

Alicia Says:

"I always want to stay focused on who I am, even as I'm discovering who I am."

Alicia fell in love with playing the piano when she was young. She says it helped her get through some difficult times.

FINDING FAME

Things started to move fast. Alicia performed her first single "Fallin'" on *Oprah*. It was one day before the album was released. Thanks to the show's large audience, many people heard her sound. They liked it! The album won five Grammy Awards including Song of the Year. Her next album, *Diary of Alicia Keys*, was released in

Alicia Keys and record producer Clive Davis. He heard her sound and knew it was special.

2003. It won three Grammys. Alicia also made time for the theater. In 2007, she acted in the movie *Smokin' Aces*. That same year she released her third album, *As I Am*.

Alicia often opens her shows with classical piano pieces.

CHAPTER 3
A NEW PASSION

Alicia had first become aware of AIDS (acquired immunodeficiency syndrome) at a young age. When she was eight years old, a family friend had died from the disease. New York had been one of the cities hardest hit by AIDS.

In 2003, Alicia met AIDS activist Leigh Blake. She had spent years working in Africa. The AIDS crisis there was worse than what New York had been through. Leigh told Alicia about the mothers she met in places like Kenya, Rwanda, and South Africa. They could not afford AIDS medicine for their sick children.

SPREADING KNOWLEDGE

Together, Alicia and Leigh traveled to South Africa. They filmed a Staying Alive documentary for MTV.

Alicia Says:

"It's important to talk to our kids about having compassion and not ostracizing people who are infected or affected by AIDS."

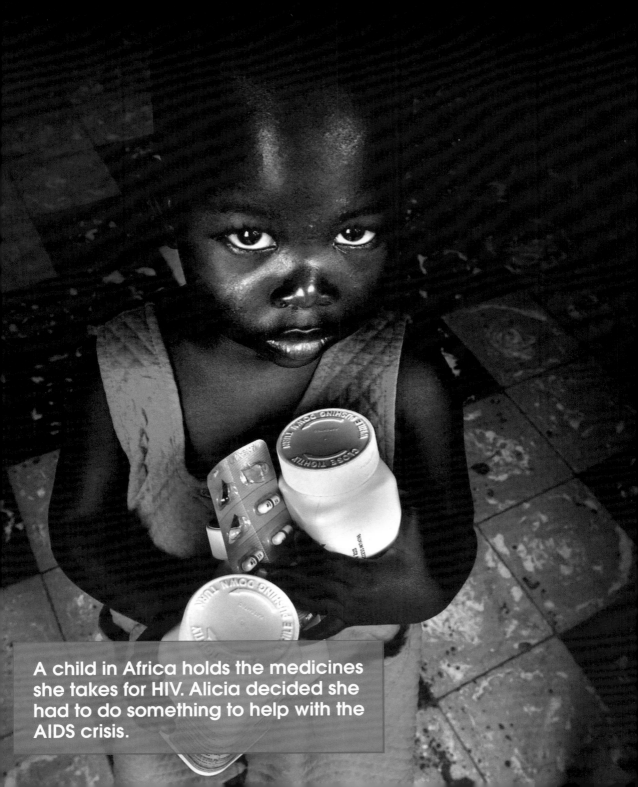

A child in Africa holds the medicines she takes for HIV. Alicia decided she had to do something to help with the AIDS crisis.

They wanted to teach people about AIDS. They visited pregnant women, mothers, and children living with the disease. Alicia saw many poor people who could not get the medical care they needed. She felt angry. She also felt motivated.

WORKING FOR CHANGE

Alicia knew she had to act. Together with Leigh Blake she helped start Keep a Child Alive (KCA). The group's goal

Alicia teamed up with Bono to raise money for Keep a Child Alive. Here they are at a concert in 2007.

Alicia speaks about Keep a Child Alive in 2016.

Alicia Keys and Bono recorded a cover of the Peter Gabriel song "Don't Give Up" to raise money for Keep a Child Alive.

is to treat, care for, and support children and families affected by HIV/AIDS. Alicia became the KCA Global **Ambassador**. She also sponsors children by donating help and health care. In 2014, she hosted the KCA's Black Ball. The event raised nearly $2.4 million.

CHAPTER 4
COLLABORATIONS

Alicia was ready for her next adventure. This time she wasn't alone. In 2008, she met a musician named Kasseem Dean. His stage name is Swizz Beatz. They fell in love and married in July 2010 on the French island of Corsica. In October, their first son, Egypt Daoud Dean, was born. Their second son, Genesis Ali Dean, was born in December 2014.

Alicia and her husband, Swizz Beatz, attend an event with their son Egypt.

SPEAKING OUT

As Alicia grew, her sound matured as well. Today she continues to find ways to combine her creative talents with her strong personal beliefs. In 2017, she was a key speaker at the Women's March on Washington. The march drew nearly half a million people. People around the world were part of the

Alicia speaks out at the Women's March on Washington in 2017.

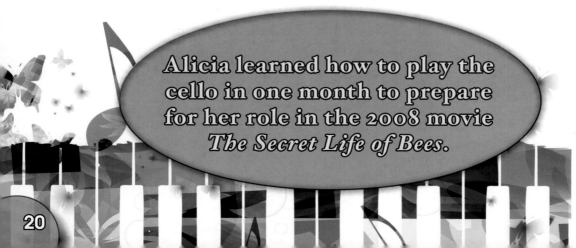

Alicia learned how to play the cello in one month to prepare for her role in the 2008 movie *The Secret Life of Bees.*

protest. They called for laws to protect **human rights** and other issues.

ALICIA'S MESSAGE

Alicia saw the march as a way to use her talent to fight for a better world for her children and everyone else. She told the crowd: "We are mothers. We are caregivers. We are artists. We are activists. We are **entrepreneurs**, doctors, leaders of industry and technology. Our potential is unlimited. We rise." Alicia is dedicated to her dream, and she stays true to herself. These qualities have allowed her star to rise as well.

> **Alicia Says:**
> "**We value education, health care, equality.**"

TIMELINE

1981 Alicia Augello Cook is born in Hell's Kitchen, New York City, on January 25.

1998 Signs with Arista Records.
Receives a scholarship from Columbia University.

1999 Leaves Arista for J Records.

2001 First album, *Songs in A Minor*, debuts.

2002 *Songs in A Minor* wins five Grammy Awards.

2003 Second album, *Diary of Alicia Keys*, debuts at number one.
Alicia and AIDS activist Leigh Blake form Keep a Child Alive.

2010 Marries Kasseem Dean.
Son Egypt Daoud Dean is born.

2014 Wins her fifteenth Grammy Award for R&B album *Girl on Fire*.
Son Genesis Ali Dean is born.

2017 Speaks and performs at the Women's March on Washington.

LEARN MORE

BOOKS

Helsby, Genevieve. *My First Piano Book*. Franklin, TN: Naxos, 2018.

Shea, Molly. *Alicia Keys*. New York, NY: Gareth Stevens, 2011.

Simons, Rae. *A Kid's Guide to AIDS and HIV*. Vestal, NY: Village Earth Press, 2016.

WEBSITES

Alicia Keys

aliciakeys.com

Alicia's official website provides fans with the latest information on the star.

Keep a Child Alive

keepachildalive.org

Learn more about Alicia's work to end HIV/AIDS.

INDEX

Published in 2019 by Enslow Publishing, LLC.
101 W. 23rd Street, Suite 240, New York, NY 10011

Library of Congress Cataloging-in-Publication Data
Names: Santos, Rita, author.
Title: Alicia Keys : singer-songwriter / Rita Santos.
Description: New York : Enslow Publishing, 2019. | Series: Junior biographies| Includes bibliographical references and index. | Audience: Grades 3-5. Identifiers: LCCN 2018007633| ISBN 9781978502055 (library bound) | ISBN 9781978502352 (pbk.) | ISBN 9781978502369 (6 pack)
Subjects: LCSH: Keys, Alicia–Juvenile literature. | Singers–United States–Biography–Juvenile literature. | Rhythm and blues musicians–United States–Biography–Juvenile literature.
Classification: LCC ML3930.K39 S26 2018 | DDC 782.42164092 [B] –dc23
LC record available at https://lccn.loc.gov/2018007633

Printed in the United States of America

To Our Readers: We have done our best to make sure all website addresses in this book were active and appropriate when we went to press. However, the author and the publisher have no control over and assume no liability for the material available on those websites or on any websites they may link to. Any comments or suggestions can be sent by e-mail to customerservice@enslow.com.

Photos Credits: Cover, p. 1 Presley Ann/Patrick McMullan/Getty Images; pp. 2, 3, 22, 23, 24, back cover (curves graphic) Alena Kazlouskaya/Shutterstock.com; p. 4 Jon Kopaloff/FilmMagic /Getty Images; pp. 6, 17 Kevin Mazur/Child/WireImage /Getty Images; p. 8 Jeff Greenberg/Photolibrary/Getty Images; p. 11 Hayley Madden/Redferns/Getty Images; p. 12 Lester Cohen/WireImage/Getty Images; p. 13 Vince Bucci/Getty Images; p. 15 Ami Vitale/Getty Images; p. 16 Michael Loccisano/FilmMagic/Getty Images; p. 19 Gilbert Carrasquillo/FilmMagic/Getty Images; p. 20 Paul Morigi/WireImage/Getty Images; interior page bottoms (music notes) abstract/Shutterstock.com.